UNITED STATES
NAVY SEALS

BY JOHN HAMILTON

VISIT US AT
WWW.ABDOPUBLISHING.COM

Published by ABDO Publishing Company, 8000 West 78th Street, Suite 310, Edina, MN 55439. Copyright ©2012 by Abdo Consulting Group, Inc. International copyrights reserved in all countries. No part of this book may be reproduced in any form without written permission from the publisher. A&D Xtreme™ is a trademark and logo of ABDO Publishing Company.

Printed in the United States of America,
North Mankato, Minnesota.
062011
092011

 PRINTED ON RECYCLED PAPER

Editor: Sue Hamilton
Graphic Design: Sue Hamilton
Cover Design: John Hamilton
Cover Photo: Getty Images
Interior Photos: AP-pg 27; Corbis-pgs 8, 9, 14, 15; Dept of Defense-pgs 18 & 32; DVIDS-pgs 17, 22, 23, 28 & 29; Getty-pgs 6, 7, 10, 11, 12, 13, & 16; Navy SEALs-pgs 1-5, 7, 13 (insert), 25, 26, & 30-32; Office of Strategic Services-pg 8 (insert); US Navy-pgs 19, 20, 21, & 24.

Library of Congress Cataloging-in-Publication Data

Hamilton, John, 1959-
  Navy SEALs / John Hamilton.
    p. cm. -- (United States Armed Forces)
  Includes index.
  Audience: Ages 8-15.
  ISBN 978-1-61783-067-9
  1. United States. Navy. SEALs--Juvenile literature. 2. United States. Navy--Commando troops--Juvenile literature. I. Title.
  VG87.H36 2012
  359.9'84--dc23
                              2011020556

CONTENTS

XTREME FACT
Navy SEALs currently have about 2,000 members.

NAVY SEALS

Navy SEALs are the elite special operations soldiers of the United States Navy. They take their name from the elements in which they operate: sea, air, and land. SEALs perform some of the most dangerous missions of all special operations forces.

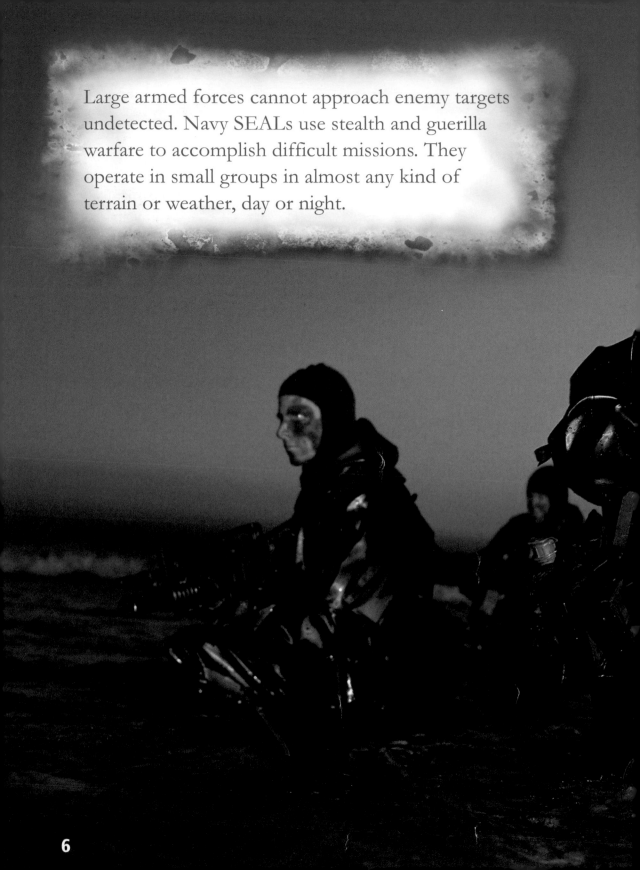

Large armed forces cannot approach enemy targets undetected. Navy SEALs use stealth and guerilla warfare to accomplish difficult missions. They operate in small groups in almost any kind of terrain or weather, day or night.

SEALs are especially known for their skill in underwater missions.

HISTORY

The United States Navy used underwater commandos during World War II. Sailors who were expert swimmers formed underwater demolition teams. These "frogmen" destroyed enemy obstacles, clearing the way for amphibious beach landings. They fought against Germany during the D-Day invasion of Normandy, France, and in many islands of the Pacific Ocean in the fight against Japan.

A frogman from 1944.

An underwater explosion is set off by a demolitions team training in Virginia in 1947.

Today's Navy SEALs were officially formed in 1962. President John F. Kennedy knew that modern warfare required special operations units, which are small, stealthy groups that fight in enemy territory. The first SEALs came from Navy underwater demolition teams.

SEALs earned their fierce reputation during the Vietnam War in the 1960s and early 1970s. They fought along the shores, rivers, and jungles of Vietnam. Missions included spying on the enemy, ambushing supplies and troops, and sabotaging bridges and communications sites.

In 1967, Navy SEALs come ashore for a mission in South Vietnam.

TRAINING

SEAL trainees build endurance by holding a log nicknamed "Misery" over their heads. Instructors tell recruits that Misery loves company.

XTREME FACT
SEAL trainees learn many skills, including demolition, martial arts, marksmanship, parachuting, and teamwork.

Freezing in cold ocean water, SEAL trainees learn how much they can withstand.

SEALs are men chosen from the U.S. Navy or Coast Guard. Training is a grueling ordeal. It can take as long as 30 months—two and a half years—before a SEAL is ready for deployment. Only about 20 percent of SEALs make it through training. Trainees are pushed to the limit, both physically and mentally. They undergo similar stresses they would encounter in actual battle.

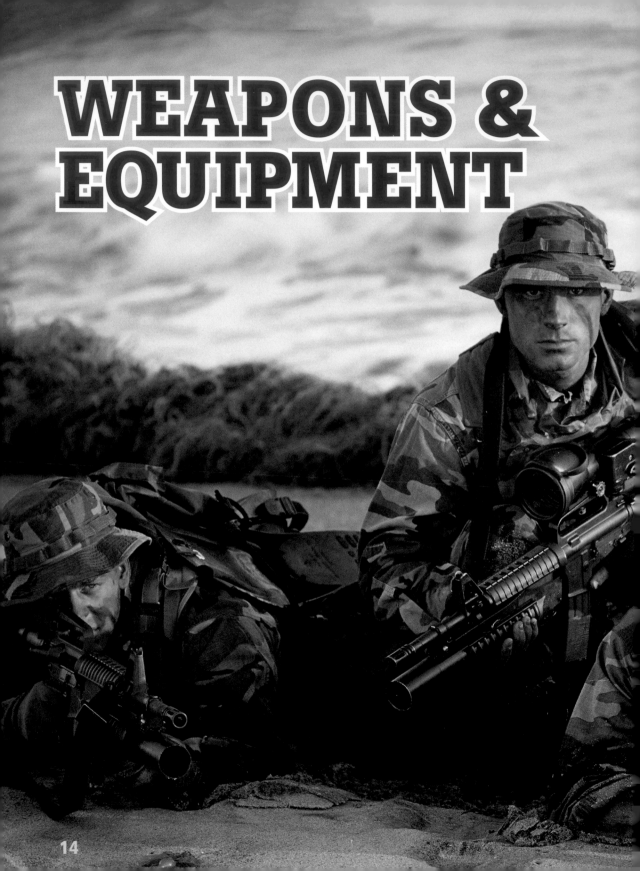

WEAPONS & EQUIPMENT

Navy SEALs use a variety of weapons, depending on the situations they expect to find on their combat missions. SEALs often carry rifles with short barrels so they can maneuver in tight spaces, such as doorways and vehicles. Common weapons include the M4 carbine assault rifle and HK MP5 9mm submachine gun. The M4 can also be outfitted with a grenade launcher under the barrel. Suppressors reduce a weapon's noise. This keeps nearby enemies from being alerted to the team's presence.

SEALs often operate under cover of darkness. Night vision goggles give the SEALs a huge battlefield advantage. SEALs can communicate using advanced satellite technology. Their radio signals are encrypted to prevent the enemy from intercepting them. Helmet cameras transmit real-time battlefield video to commanders back at base.

A Navy SEAL wears night vision goggles as he prepares to go on a mission.

Night vision allows SEALs to see in the dark. SEAL trainees are seen here carrying an inflatable boat.

XTREME FACT
A flashbang is a stun grenade that produces a bright light and loud noise, temporarily disorienting the enemy.

SEA MISSIONS

SEALs use scuba gear, special boats, or underwater vehicles launched from submarines to get to their objectives. SEAL combat swimmers are experts in underwater demolitions. They can blow up boats or remove obstacles from harbors and rivers.

Some missions require the use of Combat Rubber Raiding Crafts (CRRC) to transport SEALs quickly to enemy shores.

SEAL Delivery Vehicles (SDV) carry combat swimmers and their equipment long distances into enemy territory. They are often launched from the backs of submarines. SEALs breath using the vehicle's air supply, or by using their own scuba gear.

SEALs emerge from the sea in small teams, often sneaking into enemy territory at night. They can deploy almost anywhere in the world. They work quietly, conducting sensitive and important missions that require stealth, speed, and initiative.

AIR MISSIONS

When attacking from the sea isn't an option, SEALs often use aircraft to reach mission targets. They may fast-rope using a 50- to 90-foot (15- to 27-m) rope that dangles from a hovering helicopter.

SEALs can also parachute from high-flying airplanes. Staying in a tight group during a jump requires much precision.

LAND MISSIONS

When operating on land, SEALs are trained to drive almost any kind of vehicle. They are expert navigators. They even climb in mountainous terrain. One of the SEALs' most important missions is reconnaissance. They secretly gather information about the enemy in order to help regular U.S. ground troops. Other missions include sabotaging enemy targets, and training and supplying foreign fighters friendly to the United States.

A SEAL operates a Desert Patrol Vehicle (DPV). The dune buggy is made for harsh desert terrain, and comes with superior communication and weapons systems.

SEAL snipers are trained to use appropriate camouflage for any environment.

SEAL TEAM SIX

SEAL Team Six is a super-secret unit that is used on especially sensitive or hazardous missions. Its official name is the United States Naval Special Warfare Development Group (DEVGRU). Most SEAL Team Six missions are highly classified, and are seldom commented on by the military or the White House.

On May 1, 2011, members of SEAL Team Six helicoptered to a large house in the city of Abbottabad, Pakistan, under cover of darkness. In an attack that lasted just 38 minutes, the SEALs searched the house and compound for the world's most-wanted man, Osama bin Laden. He was the founder of the terrorist organization al-Qaeda, the group responsible for the September 11, 2001, attacks against the United States. During the fight, bin Laden was killed. The military reported that no SEAL team members were injured.

THE FUTURE

In the past 50 years, Navy SEALs have fought in many war-torn places worldwide. They have fought in Grenada, Panama, Somalia, and the Persian Gulf. Navy SEALs have been used in many operations in the War on Terror, including missions in Iraq, Afghanistan, and Pakistan.

Navy SEALs are among the best-trained fighters in the world. Their missions are dangerous and top secret. The world will never know the accomplishments of many SEALs. But they stand ready to protect the United States whenever they are called.

GLOSSARY

AMPHIBIOUS
Operating on both land and water.

COMMANDO
Commandos are highly trained soldiers who specialize in raids, sometimes using techniques such as rappelling or parachuting to reach their targets. Commandos often use stealth to attack the enemy. They are also sometimes used to rescue hostages.

FAST-ROPE
A troop-insertion technique where soldiers descend a thick rope that hangs from a helicopter. Fast-roping is required for places where helicopters cannot land, or there is too much enemy activity for them to land.

Troops use gloves and slide down the rope, using their hands to control their descent. The technique can be very dangerous, especially if a soldier is carrying heavy equipment.

GUERRILLA WARFARE

Small groups of combatants (sometimes including civilians) who use the element of surprise and mobility to achieve their objectives. Teams of guerillas excel at ambushes and sabotage.

SCUBA

Equipment that allows divers to breathe underwater without a hose attached to the surface or other air supply. Scuba stands for "self contained underwater breathing apparatus."

SPECIAL OPERATIONS

Military forces that use unconventional warfare. They are usually organized in small groups, and use stealth, speed, and surprise to achieve their objectives. Special operations soldiers are highly trained and self reliant while on the battlefield.

INDEX